SMALL BUT *DEADLY*

DEADLY
BLACK WIDOWS

By Greg Roza

 Gareth Stevens
Publishing

Please visit our website, www.garethstevens.com. For a free color catalog of all our high-quality books, call toll free 1-800-542-2595 or fax 1-877-542-2596.

Library of Congress Cataloging-in-Publication Data

Roza, Greg.
Deadly black widows / Greg Roza.
    p. cm.— (Small but deadly)
Includes index.
ISBN 978-1-4339-5732-1 (pbk.)
ISBN 978-1-4339-5733-8 (6-pack)
ISBN 978-1-4339-5730-7 (library binding)
1. Black widow spider—Juvenile literature. I. Title.
QL458.42.T54R69 2011
595.4′4—dc22
                                            2010047159

First Edition

Published in 2012 by
Gareth Stevens Publishing
111 East 14th Street, Suite 349
New York, NY 10003

Copyright © 2012 Gareth Stevens Publishing

Designer: Michael J. Flynn
Editor: Greg Roza

Photo credits: Cover, pp. 1, (cover, back cover, 2–4, 7–8, 11–12, 15–16, 19–24 background texture), 7, 13 (all), 17, 20 Shutterstock.com; pp. 5, 6, 9, 10, 14 iStockphoto; p. 18 George Grall/National Geographic/Getty Images.

Printed in the United States of America

CPSIA compliance information: Batch #CS11GS: For further information contact Gareth Stevens, New York, New York at 1-800-542-2595.

CONTENTS

Words in the glossary appear in **bold** type the first time they are used in the text.

MEET THE BLACK WIDOW

There are several kinds of black widow spiders, and they can be found throughout the world. They prefer areas that are warm for at least part of the year. They're found throughout the United States, but they're most common in the deserts of the American Southwest.

Black widows are venomous spiders. This means they make a deadly liquid called venom inside their bodies. They use this venom to kill **prey** and scare away **predators**.

DEADLY DATA

The black widow is the most venomous spider in North America.

Black widows have eight eyes arranged in two rows of four each. However, they can't see very well.

Living close to the ground puts black widows in danger. They often get stepped on.

BLACK WIDOW HABITATS

Black widows like warm places, but they live in many different **habitats**. They can be found in forests, jungles, deserts, and grasslands. Sometimes they're found living near people—in sheds, barns, or woodpiles. They may even creep inside if it gets too cold outside!

Unlike many other spiders, most black widows don't spin webs high off the ground. They mainly live close to the ground. Black widows like to hide in hollow logs, in bushes, and under loose rocks.

THE LONELY LIFE

Black widows live alone. They come together only to **mate**. They're most active at night. Black widows build their webs in cool, dark areas. Once they have built a web, they hang upside down in a special part of it. They spend much of their time waiting for bugs to get trapped in their webs. If a larger animal bothers its web, the black widow usually runs and hides. Outside of their webs, black widows are **clumsy** animals.

DEADLY DATA

Female black widows sometimes kill
and eat the males after mating!

Female black widows spend most of their lives hanging upside down in their webs.

9

The hourglass shape on the female black widow is a warning to other animals.

male

female

FEMALES AND MALES

A female black widow's body is round, black, and shiny. Most have a yellow or red hourglass shape on their body. The female's body is about the size of a pea, but the spider can be about 1.5 inches (3.8 cm) long with its legs spread out.

The male's body isn't as round as the female's body. Its legs are much longer than its body. The male has red and white stripes and shapes on its body and legs.

DEADLY DATA

A male black widow is only about one-half the size of a female.

GROWING UP

A female black widow lays several bunches, or sacs, of eggs at one time. She wraps the eggs with silk to keep them safe. Each egg sac can hold up to 750 eggs!

Shortly after they come out of the egg sacs, baby black widows leave the web. They let out a long piece of silk and float away with the wind. This is called ballooning. Female black widows can live up to 3 years. Males **mature** faster than females, but they only live for about 3 to 4 months.

DEADLY DATA

Males leave right after mating. They don't help guard the eggs.

egg sac

Young black widows all look like the adult male.

The tips of a black widow's legs are oily. This keeps the spider from getting caught in its own web.

WIDOW WEBS

Black widow silk is stronger than most spider silk. Female black widows build large, strong webs. Their webs look tangled and messy. This type of web is called a cobweb. Black widow webs often have a hollow area inside them. This is where the female spends most of her time.

Males make smaller webs between the time they leave their mother's web and the time they are ready to mate. They don't stay in them for long.

DEADLY DATA

A black widow feels its web shake when prey becomes trapped in it.

TRAPPED!

Black widows eat many kinds of bugs, including flies, cockroaches, and spiders. They'll even eat other black widows! Their tangled webs are perfect for trapping bugs that crawl into them.

Black widows are sometimes called comb-footed spiders. This is because their back legs have hairs on them, which make them look like combs. They use these legs to toss silk quickly over their prey. Soon, the prey can't move and is ready to be eaten.

DEADLY DATA

Black widows prefer to eat live prey. However, they'll eat dead prey if they can't find anything else.

This black widow is wrapping up an unlucky grasshopper that got caught in its web.

fangs

Black widow bites don't often kill people, but they can be very painful.

BLACK WIDOW VENOM

Black widow venom is very strong. Although male black widows are venomous, there are no reported cases of them biting people. Young black widows aren't venomous.

Once a black widow has its prey wrapped in silk, the spider bites it with its **fangs**. The spider shoots something into the prey's body that turns its insides to liquid. Then the black widow sucks out the liquid. When the spider is done feeding, the prey is just an empty shell!

DEADLY DATA

Black widow venom is said to be about 15 times stronger than rattlesnake venom. However, the spider delivers much less venom in a single bite.

PEOPLE AND BLACK WIDOWS

Most black widow bites happen when people sit or step on the spider. A bite feels like a pinprick. The venom causes swelling and redness. After about 15 minutes, stomach or chest pain occurs. Other results include trouble breathing, headache, and throwing up. Very few bites result in death. Children, sick people, and old people are in the most danger.

Black widows don't present nearly as much danger as people once thought. In fact, they can be very helpful to people!

OUR FRIEND, THE BLACK WIDOW

Black widows eat bugs, such as grasshoppers and **locusts**, that destroy crops.

Black widows eat bugs, such as flies and mosquitoes, that carry illnesses.

Black widows eat bugs, such as beetles and caterpillars, that eat the leaves off trees.

In the future, black widow venom might be used to create **pesticides** and **medicines**.

Scientists believe that studying black widow silk may help them make newer, stronger ropes and clothing—maybe even lightweight, bulletproof vests!

GLOSSARY

clumsy: not moving easily or smoothly

fang: a long, pointed tooth

habitat: the place in which an animal lives

locust: a bug much like a grasshopper

mate: to come together to make babies

mature: to become an adult

medicine: a drug used to treat an illness

pesticide: something used to kill pests, such as bugs

predator: an animal that hunts and kills other animals for food

prey: an animal hunted by other animals

FOR MORE INFORMATION

BOOKS

Britton, Tamara L. *Black Widow Spiders.* Edina, MN: ABDO Publishing, 2011.

Lunis, Natalie. *Deadly Black Widows.* New York, NY: Bearport Publishing, 2009.

WEBSITES

Black Widow Spider
animals.nationalgeographic.com/animals/bugs/black-widow-spider.html
Read more about this venomous spider.

Hey! A Black Widow Spider Bit Me!
kidshealth.org/kid/ill_injure/bugs/black_widow.html
Read more about the black widow, including information about what to do if one bites you.

INDEX